Contents

Words in the text in **bold** type are explained in the Useful Words section on page 23.

Machines

Machines are any **tools**
that help people to do work.
A wheel is a machine.
Cars, lorries and bicycles
all move on wheels.
Wheels help people travel faster
and move loads further.

Axles

Axles are the bars that go
through the centre of many wheels.
Motorcycles and bicycles have two axles,
one for each wheel.
Each axle on a skateboard
holds two wheels.
Cars have two axles,
one for the front wheels,
and one for the back wheels.

Wheels move other wheels

Wheels can move other wheels.
Drivers use steering wheels
to turn the two front wheels
of cars and lorries.
Like other wheels,
steering wheels turn on an axle.

Gears

A gear is a wheel with teeth along its edge.
When gears are put side by side,
the teeth from one gear fit between
the teeth of the other gear.
Inside a watch, gears of different sizes
move the watch's hands.

Clockwise and anti-clockwise

Wheels turn either **clockwise**
or **anti-clockwise.**
When gears fit together,
they move in different directions.
If one gear moves clockwise,
the other gear moves anti-clockwise.

Sprockets

A bicycle has two or more gears
called **sprockets**.
They are connected by a chain.
Sprockets of different sizes
move the bicycle at different speeds.
Large sprockets turn a wheel slowly.
Small sprockets turn a wheel fast.
A cyclist uses more effort
to turn large sprockets.

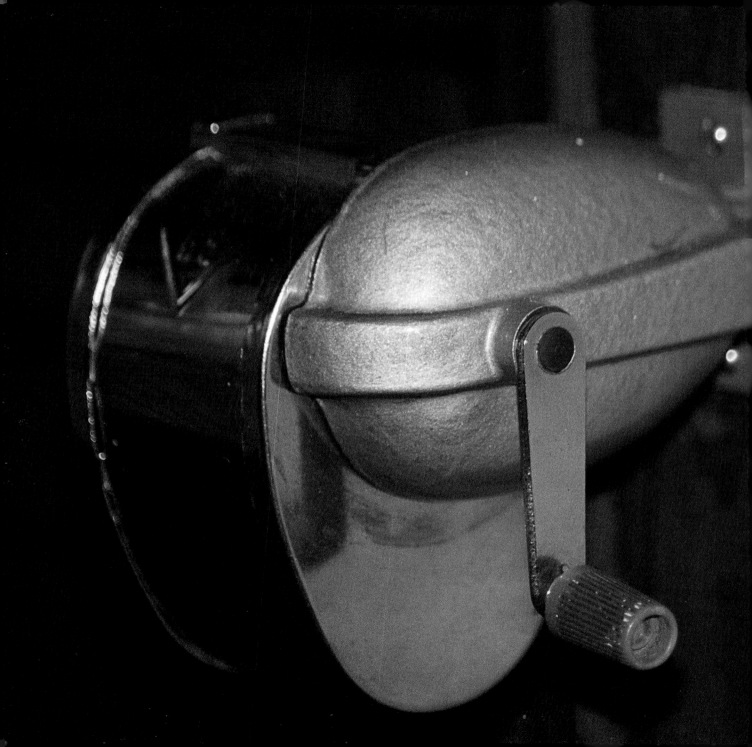

Cranks

Cranks are part of many machines.
They are a type of wheel.
Like wheels, cranks turn around an axle.
The handle of a pencil sharpener
is a crank.
A bicycle pedal is also a crank.

Cams

Cams are oblong wheels.
They can move things up and down
or backwards and forwards.
Some toys have small cams
to make them wobble across the floor.
A car's engine cannot run
without a **camshaft**.

Wheels work together

An egg whisk has
several wheels and axles
that work together.
The whisk's handle is a crank
that turns a gear.
This gear turns two small gears
that spin the whisk's beaters.
When a tool
uses many simple machines together,
it is called a **compound machine**.

Make your own wheel

Some wheels use metal balls to spin better. The balls are called bearings and look like marbles. They are used inside the wheels of skateboards and bicycles.

What you need
- Eight to ten marbles
- Lids from two jars, one bigger than the other
- Plastic plate

What you do
1 Put the smaller lid upside down on a table.
2 Fill it with marbles.
3 Put the larger lid over the marbles. The larger lid should cover the smaller one. Make sure the marbles stop the large lid touching the table.
4 Put the plate on the larger lid.
5 Gently spin the plate clockwise or anti-clockwise.

The plate is a wheel and so are the lids and the marbles. This is a compound machine because many wheels are working together.
It works like the wheels of skateboard or a bicycle.

Useful words

anti-clockwise   the opposite of clockwise

camshaft   axle with more than one cam

clockwise   the direction in which the hands
of a clock move

compound machine   one machine that is made up of
many simple machines

sprocket   a kind of gear with big teeth made to move
on a chain

tool   something a person uses to do a job

Books to read

Dixon, Malcolm and **Smith, Karen**, *Forces and Movement*,
Evans, 1997

Ollerenshaw, Chris and **Triggs, Pat**, *Gears*, Black, 1995

Turvey, Peter, *The X-Ray Picture Book of Everyday Things*,
Watts, 1995

Young, Jay, *The Amazing Science Pop-Up Book*, Watts 1995

Index

PRINTED IN BELGIUM BY
proost
INTERNATIONAL BOOK PRODUCTION